Looking at Europe

Estonia

Piret Hiisjärv
Ene Hiiepuu

The Oliver Press, Inc.
Minneapolis

This edition published in 2006 by The Oliver Press, Inc.
Charlotte Square
5707 West 36th Street
Minneapolis, MN 55416-2510
USA

Published by arrangement with KIT Publishers, The Netherlands, and
The Evans Publishing Group, London, UK, 2005

Library of Congress Cataloging-in-Publication Data

Hiisjärv, Piret.
    Estonia / Piret Hiisjärv, Ene Hiiepuu.
        p. cm. -- (Looking at Europe)
    Includes index.
    Contents: History -- The country -- Towns and cities -- People and culture -- Education
-- Cuisine -- Transportation -- The economy -- Nature.
    ISBN 1-881508-32-3
    1. Estonia--Juvenile literature. I. Hiiepuu, Ene. II. Title. III. Series.

    DK503.23.H55 2006
    947.98--dc22

                                                                        2006040084

Text: Piret Hiisjärv and Ene Hiiepuu
Photographs: Jan Willem Bultje
US editing: Holly Day
Design and Layout: Grafisch Ontwerpbureau Agaatsz BNO, Meppel, The Netherlands
Cover: Icon Productions, Minneapolis, USA
Cartography: Armand Haye, Amsterdam, The Netherlands
Production: J & P Far East Productions, Soest, The Netherlands

Picture Credits
All images courtesy of KIT Publishers except:
p. 25(b) © CORBIS SYGMA; p. 39(m) © Attal Serge/CORBIS SYGMA; 39(b) © Attal Serge/
CORBIS SYGMA

ISBN 1-881508-32-3
Printed in Singapore
10 09 08 07 06   8 7 6 5 4 3 2 1

Contents

CSCL

Introduction

The Republic of Estonia is located in north-central Europe. It is one of the Baltic states along the coast of the Baltic Sea. Estonia borders the Gulf of Finland in the north, Russia in the east, Latvia in the south, the Gulf of Riga in the southwest, and the Baltic Sea in the west.

Estonia also includes several hundred small islands off the coast. Although the country lies in northern Europe, its temperature is quite mild because so much of it is bordered by the sea, which moderates the climate. Much of the interior landscape is lowland, dotted with many lakes that were left over from the last Ice Age.

Estonian language and culture is closely linked to Scandinavia. Estonia's history, however, has been more closely intertwined with Russia, despite being ruled by Germans, Swedes and Danes at different times in its history. In 1721, Estonia came under Russian rule, and except for a brief period of independence between the two world wars, it remained so until the 1990s. The Russian influence can still be felt all over the country, and thousands of Russian people live in Estonia.

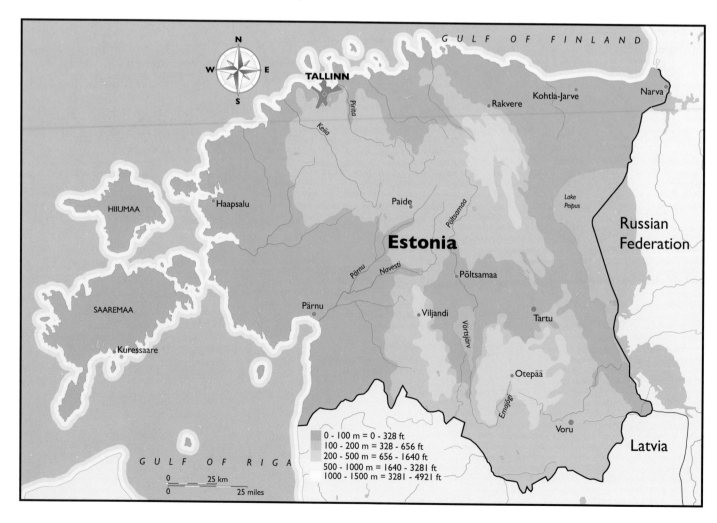

Estonia was granted full independence in 1991, one of the first countries to declare its freedom after the collapse of the communist Soviet Union. Since then, it has been rebuilding its economy and other infrastructures that had suffered during the years of foreign rule. A constitution was established in 1992, making Estonia a parliamentary republic, governed from the capital Tallinn.

Independence has allowed the Estonian people to revive many ancient traditions that had been suppressed for centuries. Today they celebrate their heritage with great enthusiasm, in the use of their own language, the staging of festivals, and the revival of many old customs.

Over the past decade, Estonia has concentrated on strengthening international relations by joining several organizations, including the United Nations, the World Trade Organization and UNESCO. It became a full member of the European Union in May 2004, and this has provided the country with much support in the processes of stabilizing and restructuring.

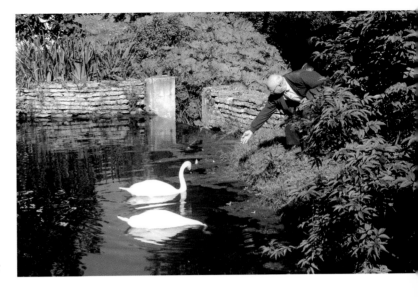

▲ *There are thousands of lakes and ponds in Estonia.*

▼ *Large parts of Estonia are devoted to agriculture, and this remains an important industry. Fields of rye like this one are interspersed with cornflowers — one of Estonia's national symbols.*

History

The first people to inhabit Estonia arrived there about 10,000 years ago. The earliest settlement grew up in the western part of the country around 7500 BC. However, the ancestors of present-day Estonians are believed to have been hunters who arrived from parts of northern Europe between 3000 and 2000 BC.

▼ *The ancient Estonians buried their dead in stone coffins that were covered with limestone plates and surrounded by circular stone walls. Some of these graves can still be seen today at Jõelähtme, near Tallinn.*

At that time, Estonian territory was covered with forests and swamps, and the ancient peoples founded small communities around lakes and along river banks. The men hunted wild animals and fished, while the women picked berries and whatever else the forests offered. They made tools out of stones, bones and wood. Later, merchants from neighboring lands ventured into the territory and taught the people how to process metal, so they began making tools from bronze. Gradually, raising livestock became an increasingly common way of earning a living and providing food.

▶ *A citadel was a fortified town built on a hill or a swamp island. Its inner courtyard was surrounded by a high mound and strong wooden walls. Later, stone was used instead of wood. This is the fortress of Rakvere in northern Estonia.*

By the first century BC, the use of bronze in tool- and weapon-making had given way to iron, which was much stronger and more durable. Iron tools made it easier to cut down trees for wood and to cultivate farmland. Plowing the land and growing crops became widespread practices, and more and more people settled in one place. Gradually, small villages expanded to form parishes and parishes joined to form counties. The Estonian people were good at handicrafts, and they made everything they needed, from buildings to tools and clothes.

Throughout this time, the Estonians had largely lived in peace, without being threatened by invasion and conquest. However, by the sixth century, increasing numbers of foreigners were entering the territory, particularly the Slavs and Vikings. The Estonians started building fortified strongholds and citadels to protect themselves from invaders. Despite these threats, the Estonians built up good trading relationships with their neighbors. Merchants exchanged materials such as salt, iron, amber and tools for flax, honey, animal skins, grain, and wax.

The Christian Crusades

By the end of the twelfth century, most European nations had converted to Christianity. The people of Finland and the Baltic states, including Estonia, were the only ones still following pagan rituals and beliefs. The pope organized a crusade with the aim of bringing Christianity to the Baltic nations. The crusades lasted from 1208 to 1227, and during this time the Estonians were treated harshly and forced to adopt Christianity against their will. One result of the campaign was that the Baltic lands were divided between German crusaders and Danish invaders. In some areas, small independent principalities were formed, including Livonia, which covered most of Estonia. The conquered countries were dedicated to the Virgin Mary, and Estonia is still sometimes referred to as "Mary's Land" (Maarjamaa).

The ancient Estonians believed that every animal, bird, tree, stone and plant had a soul. They thought that fairies lived in houses and mermaids inhabited the water. Water from fresh springs flowing from the earth was believed to have healing properties. Fire had a cleansing purpose – the people believed that light from a bonfire would scare away evil forces, especially at the times of equinoxes, when day and night are of equal length. Even today, Estonians maintain the tradition of jumping over a bonfire during the autumn equinox.

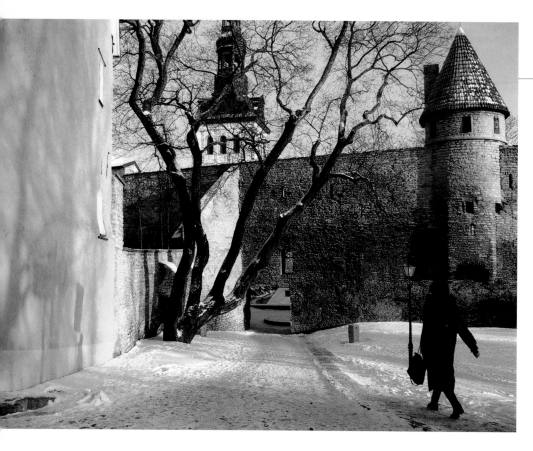

◀ In the Middle Ages, Livonia had several key towns, all of which were surrounded by high walls, and had very narrow streets and multi-story buildings. Of all the medieval towns in Estonia, the capital, Tallinn, is the best-preserved, with many churches, a town hall and merchants' courtyards.

The Middle Ages

By the Middle Ages, people of several nationalities were living in Estonian territories. The Germans were the most powerful, and made up the land-owning classes, the clergy, and town leaders. There were also some Russian merchants in the towns and cities. Livonian towns belonged to the powerful political Hanseatic League, and a lot of trade took place between Livonia and Russia. The native Estonians lived as peasants, working for powerful landlords. A landlord's property was divided into two sections. Part was "manor land," where the peasants worked for the lord of the manor for a certain number of days each year, using their own tools and animals. The second part was farmland, which was rented to peasants for their own use. Some of the harvest was paid to the landlord as rent.

▶ Many stone churches, castles and citadels for different monastic orders were built in the countryside. The Padise monastery was constructed between 1305 and 1317, and has been destroyed and rebuilt several times during the course of its history.

The Estonian peasants had hardly any rights in the Middle Ages. They were serfs – the lowest social class – until the sixteenth century, and were not even allowed to leave their houses without the permission of their landlord.

During this time, Estonian lands were the site of several conflicts. Polish and Swedish troops occupied the country during the Livonian War (1558–83), after which Sweden gained control of Estonia. In the Great Northern War (1700–21), Estonia was invaded by Russia. This marked the beginning of the rule of the Russian tsars, which lasted for 200 years.

Although they were still ruled by foreigners, this period marked a change in fortunes for the Estonian people. In the time of Swedish rule, a network of public schools was established, providing basic education and training for farmers. King Gustav Adolf II founded the University of Tartu in southeast Estonia in 1632. This was the first institute for higher education in the country, although most students were German, Swedish, or Finnish.

▼ *The University of Tartu is the oldest institute of higher education in Estonia, dating from the seventeenth century.*

◄ At the open-air museum near Tallinn, many old houses and farmhouses have been preserved and can be seen as they would have looked in medieval times.

Life was still not easy for the Estonians. Until the end of the nineteenth century, most of them lived in the barns and sheds where grain was threshed and stored. These were made of pine wood, clay, and stone, with hay or reed roofs. Country houses looked a lot like normal farms. Towards the end of the eighteenth century, landowners started developing rural estates, copying the styles they had seen during travels abroad. These estates were often surrounded by parks that contained pavilions and artificial lakes.

National awakening

Throughout these years of oppression, the Estonians always remembered their own heritage, and were determined that one day they would regain the land they had lost. At the beginning of the nineteenth century, many farmers rebelled against their landlords and, in 1819, serfdom was abolished. By the middle of the century, Estonian people were allowed to buy their own houses. The national awakening that would eventually lead to independence had begun.

In the nineteenth century, efforts were being made to increase knowledge of the Bible, and in Estonia this resulted in a rise in literacy. New schools were established and books were printed. Even farmers were allowed to receive an education. The first Estonian to graduate was Friedrich Robert Faehlmann, author of the epic poem *Kalevipoeg*.

▶ The Vanemuine was the first theater to open in Estonia.

The first Estonian national weekly magazine was published in 1857. In 1865, the first amateur theater was established, the Vanemuine. In time, this developed into a professional theater, performing pieces in the Estonian language. By 1880, 85 percent of the population was literate. However, the same year, the Russians began to assert their authority over the Baltic states and Russian became the official language in all schools. Despite this, the Estonians maintained and strengthened their national customs.

The National Movement gained momentum in the early years of the twentieth century. The Russian Revolution in 1917 provided Estonia and the other Baltic countries with an opportunity to seize independence, and the following year the Republic of Estonia was created. It was formally established by the Tartu Peace Treaty in 1920. For the next 20 years, Estonia enjoyed a rapidly growing economy and a great surge in national culture.

▼ *The magnificent house on the Palmse estate, where the noble family Von der Pahlen lived. Palmse shows how very different the lives of the foreign ruling classes were from those of the Estonian peasant farmers.*

The Second World War

The Second World War began in 1939. Germany and the Soviet Union signed an agreement – the Molotov-Ribbentrop Pact – in which Estonia fell under the rule of the Soviets. In 1940, Soviet troops marched into and occupied Estonia, claiming that the country had "voluntarily" agreed to become a state in the Soviet Union. More than 60,000 Estonians were deported or killed in the first year of Soviet occupation.

In 1941, the Germans went back on their word and invaded Soviet Russia and the Baltic countries. Many Estonians saw the German troops as liberators from the Soviet regime and fought on their side during the invasion. For the next three years, Estonia was ruled by Germany, and it was only in 1944 that the Soviets re-occupied Estonia. Their revenge on the local people was harsh, and many Estonians fled abroad. Those who remained were forced to give up their land and livestock. All businesses fell under Soviet state control. Russian was declared the official language once again.

The Soviet government established an industrial network that attracted many Russians to Estonia. The number of natives in the country continued to decline after the war ended in 1945, and by 1989, only 61.5 percent of the population was Estonian.

▲ *The articles of the Molotov-Ribbentrop Pact, a non-aggression treaty between Germany and the Soviet Union, in which they agreed to divide ownership of other lands. By the terms of the treaty, Estonia fell to the Soviets.*

Independence

The Soviets ruled Estonia for the next four decades. As the 1980s drew to a close, barriers between the communist East and the democratic West were being broken down all over Europe. On August 23, 1989, two million people formed a human chain stretching more than 370 miles, from Tallinn in Estonia to Vilnius in Lithuania, to demonstrate against Soviet rule. In 1990, Estonia declared its independence from the Soviet Union and in 1991 became a free republic.

▼ *In 1988, more than 100,000 people gathered at a festival to sing patriotic songs and to show the world how much they wanted to be an independent nation. It was known as the "Singing Revolution."*

The country

Estonia is a small country, just 17,400 square miles, including the islands offshore in the Baltic Sea. The largest of these are Saaremaa and Hiiumaa. The country is around 150 miles from north to south and around 215 miles from east to west. The landscape features marshy lowlands. It is mostly flat in the north, and more hilly in the south. The coastline stretches for about 2,350 miles.

Estonia is a rather low and featureless country. The highest points are not much more than 650 feet above sea level. Despite this, the countryside is diverse. Large forests, open swamps and marshes, fields, meadows and hills alternate with lowlands, valleys and hollows. Almost half of Estonia is covered with forests, many of them very old. The Estonian forest reserve is one of the largest in Europe.

Lakes and rivers

There are some 1,400 lakes in Estonia. The largest is Lake Peipsi, which has a surface area of 1,380 square miles. Peipsi is the fourth-largest lake in Europe. There are more than 7,000 rivers and streams, but only nine of them are longer than 60 miles. The longest is the Pärnu River, which stretches 90 miles across the country.

▼ *The coast in Lahemaa National Park in the north of the country, bordering the Baltic Sea*

▼ *The Jägala waterfall, in northern Estonia, is the most powerful in the country. The water falls from a height of 26 feet.*

Regions

Although Estonia is mainly a flat country, its natural environment varies across the different regions. Northern Estonia is characterized by shoals – peninsulas that reach far into the sea, creating bays and inlets. In some places, the coastal area is gently sloping, while in others, it rises like a high terrace straight up from the coastline.

▶ *The Emajõgi River is unique because it does not flow into the sea like the other rivers. Instead, it flows into lakes Vortjarv and Peipsi.*

Southern Estonia has the highest hills in the country. Suur Munamägi ("Big Egg Mountain"), which is 1,043 feet high, is the highest hill in the Baltic states. The domed landscape of southern Estonia is interspersed with a number of rivers and small lakes. Southern Estonia also contains the deepest lake – Rõuge Suurjärv (125 feet deep) – and the longest navigable river in Estonia – the Emajõgi. One of the biggest attractions in southern Estonia is the Piusa caves. These are man-made caves that used to be used for sandstone mining.

▲ *One of the many lakes in southern Estonia*

▼ *The Piusa caves, hidden in this sand quarry, are home to a colorful pillar maze which is 13 feet high. This is one of the largest hibernation areas for bats in Northern Europe.*

A traditional Estonian folktale tells of the birth of the Emajõgi River. When Grandfather created the world, it was a good place to live, but soon the animals were fighting with one another. Grandfather called all the animals together and said: "I can see that you need a king who will control you. To welcome him you must dig a deep, wide river into which all other rivers can flow. The name of the river will be Emajõgi." The animals did as grandfather told them, and he poured water into the river, gave it life with his breath and determined its course. This is how Emajõgi was created.

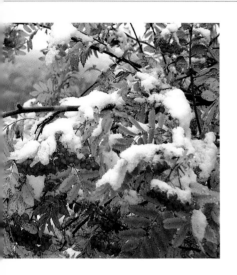

Western Estonia is a particularly low, flat region. The land is typically about 66 feet above sea level and the coastline is very ragged. The country's best-known conservation area lies in Matsalu, in western Estonia. This is an important nesting and migration place for waterfowl. Saaremaa and Hiiumaa, the country's largest islands, are also located in western Estonia. The islands are characterized by pastures with junipers, shingled coastal areas, well-preserved old houses with stone fences and thatched roofs, and windmills. The people who live on the islands observe many old customs. They wear their own traditional costumes and they speak in a dialect of the Estonian language. Several islands, including the island of Kihnu, are on the UNESCO World Heritage list.

Climate

Estonia has a moderate climate, which is influenced by its location on the Baltic Sea. The country is relatively damp, cool and windy. It can experience sudden and considerable changes in the weather. Winters are wet and summers are warm, although the heat never gets unbearable. Because Estonia is so far north, winter days are short (only six hours), but in the summer, the days are long – up to 18 hours.

The summer months in Estonia are June, July and August. The weather is warm enough to sunbathe on the beaches or to swim in the lakes or sea. In July the average temperature in Estonia is 65°F and the waters can reach temperatures of 72°F.

▲ *It is not unusual for the first snow to fall in September, but this usually melts quickly.*

▶ *Late summer and early autumn are particularly beautiful in Estonia, as the forests and bogs become cascades of color.*

Mart is sledding with his friends. "While the snow is slowly melting, we like to make snowmen, statues and castles out of snow. We have snowball fights," he explains. "Winter is fun in Estonia, because we can go skiing, skating and sledding."

Autumn begins in September. The temperature drops, and the forests and plants in the boggy areas turn into beautiful colors. Snow arrives early in Estonia, sometimes even in September. However, this first snowfall does not last long. The winter season really begins in December, and from then until February snow covers the ground. The temperatures in winter can be very changeable – from 37°F to -13°F.

▼ *The first spring flowers are usually snowdrops, which appear in late February or March.*

The spring months – March, April and May – bring a mixture of rain and sun. The inner mainland warms up faster than the sea, so the coastal areas are not as warm in spring as the rest of Estonia. However, during the summer months, the humidity in coastal regions is higher than it is inland, and therefore feels warmer.

Estonia is a wet country. Even during the summer there can be sudden downpours. In fact, the heaviest rainfall is in August. The average annual rainfall is 20–28 inches.

Towns and cities

Estonia is a small country. Only two of its cities have populations of more than 100,000 – Tallinn and Tartu. Despite this, 70 percent of the Estonian population lives in the towns and cities. The main cities are located close to the Baltic coastline. Further inland, there are mainly small towns and villages.

▼ *The first written references to Tallinn date from 1154, and many medieval monuments can still be seen in the city.*

▲ *The Kadriorg Palace was founded by Russian Tsar Peter I. Today it houses the Estonian Art Museum's foreign collection.*

Tallinn

Tallinn is the capital of Estonia and its largest city, with around 500,000 inhabitants. This is the political and cultural heart of the country, where the government buildings and embassies are located, as well as theaters, museums and many old religious buildings.

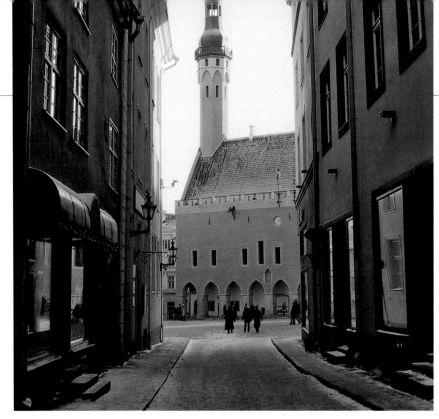

▶ *The town hall in Tallinn was built in the fourteenth century.*

Tallinn is located on the Gulf of Finland, and there has been a settlement here since at least the twelfth century. In 1219, Waldemar II of Denmark destroyed the existing town and built a fortress there. The name Tallinn comes from the Estonian *Taani linn*, which means "Danish castle." Many historical buildings survive in Tallinn, including the thirteenth-century Gothic church of St. Olai and the town hall.

Today, the city is a major Baltic port and a key industrial center for shipbuilding, manufacturing, metalworking, and food processing.

▼ *Tartu Town Hall*

Tartu

Tartu is the second-largest city in Estonia, with 105,000 inhabitants. Located in southeastern Estonia, this is the oldest town in the Baltic, founded in 1030. It is home to Tartu University, established in 1632 by Gustav Adolf II of Sweden and one of the oldest universities in Northern Europe. The oldest theater in Estonia, the Vanemuine (see page 11), can also be found here, as well as the Estonian National Museum.

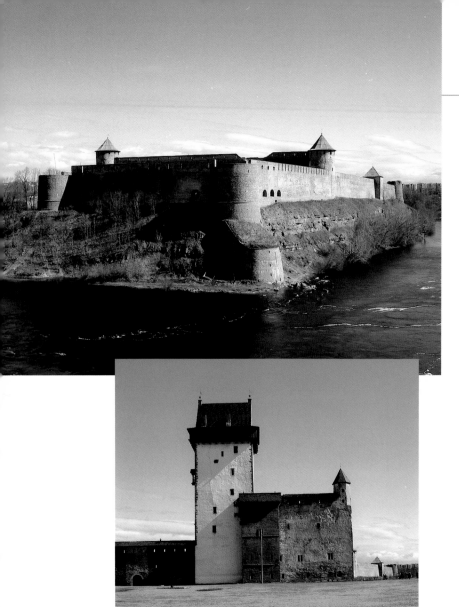

◀ Fort Ivangorod stands on the Russian side of the Narva River, overlooking the town of Narva.

Narva

Narva has around 67,000 inhabitants and lies on the border with Russia, on the banks of the Narva River. Narva was founded by the Danes in 1223 and fell to the Livonian Knights in 1346. Two fortresses stand on the banks of the Narva – Fort Ivangorod was built by Ivan III of Russia to face the Hermann Fortress built by the knights on the opposite bank.

The first battle of the Great Northern War (see page 9) was fought at Narva between the Swedes and the Russians. The Swedes won, but the town was recaptured in 1704, and remained under Russian rule until 1919.

Today, the town is a leading textile center and producer of electric power. There are several other industries in Narva, including sawmills, flax, and food-processing factories.

◀ The fifteenth-century Hermann Fortress, built by the German Livonian Knights, with its 164-foot tower

Pärnu

Pärnu is the fourth-largest town in Estonia, with around 44,000 inhabitants. It is located in the southwest of the country on the Gulf of Riga. It is widely known as the summer capital of Estonia because of its parks, white-sand beaches, and recreation centers.

The town was founded around 1250 by the Livonian Knights, and was part of the Hanseatic League. After the order of knights was dissolved in the sixteenth century, Pärnu was fought over by Sweden, Russia and Poland; it was re-incorporated into Estonia in 1918.

▶ The seaport Pärnu is a beach and health resort.

Otepää

Otepää is said to be the winter capital of Estonia because there is a great deal of snow there in the winter, which attracts skiers and other winter-sports enthusiasts. It hosts a popular annual ski marathon.

The town is located on the shores of Lake Pühajärve ("Holy Lake"), about an hour's travel south from Tartu. It was first mentioned in written documents dating from 1116, when a fortress was built here. Like many Estonian towns, it suffered during the struggles between foreigners for rule of the region. During the Great Northern War the entire area surrounding Otepää was devastated, and during the Second World War most of the town was razed to the ground by German and Russian troops.

▲ *The wooden station in Haapsalu is now a railway museum.*

Health resorts

Haapsalu is a seaside town in western Estonia. It has long been known for its warm sea waters and mud, which are believed to have health-giving properties. It became a popular health resort during the period of Russian rule, and it still attracts many visitors today.

Kuressaare is another major health resort, located on Saaremaa, the largest Estonian island. It has a well-preserved old town with narrow streets and small squares. People come here for the beaches and the health-giving mud treatments.

▶ *The Bishop's Castle in Kuressaare, dating from the fourteenth century*

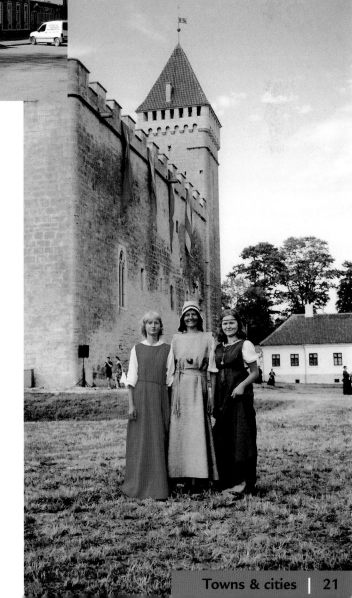

People and culture

There are around 1.3 million people living in Estonia, but only 68 percent of them are Estonians. The largest minority group is Russian (26 percent). Other ethnic groups living in Estonia include Ukrainians, Belarusians, Finns, Latvians, Poles, Lithuanians, and Germans.

▼ *The largest towns and cities, which lie around the edge of Estonia, are home to the majority of the country's population.*

The high number of Russians living in Estonia is due to the fact that until the 1990s, Estonia was under the rule of the Soviet Union. One of the most controversial decisions made after independence was limiting citizenship in the country to ethnic Estonians, which meant that inhabitants from other groups were denied many civil rights. This particularly affected the thousands of Russians living in Estonia, who were declared foreigners in 1993.

Estonia has a low population density – only 75 people per square mile, and a high proportion of these (70 percent) live in the major towns and cities.

Language

Estonian belongs to the Finno-Ugric family of languages, which also includes Finnish and Hungarian. There are believed to be as many as one million Estonian speakers all over the world. The language has no relationship to those of the other Baltic counties, Latvia and Lithuania. Although Estonian is the country's official language, 35 percent of the population speaks Russian.

Estonian uses the Latin alphabet, but some letters can be used with or without accents to indicate what kind of sound they make. A variety of dialects are still spoken in different regions. Most young people can also speak a little English.

▼ Postimees *("The Courier") has the widest circulation of any Estonian daily newspaper. Several English-language newspapers are also available in Estonia, including* The Baltic Times *and the* Tallinn City Paper.

◀ A view across Tallinn shows the church spires, including that of the Lutheran Cathedral. Several different religions exist side by side in Estonia.

Religion

Many different faiths are followed in Estonia. The constitution itself states that everyone has freedom of conscience, religion and thought.

The most widespread religion is Lutheranism – a Protestant sect, formally established in Estonia in 1686. There are also many followers of the Russian Orthodox Church because of the large numbers of Russians living in Estonia. There is an Estonian Orthodox Church as well, which was granted rights of self-government from the Russian Church in 1993. Other denominations, such as Roman Catholics, Jews, Baptists and Methodists, are also free to worship in their own churches.

▶ The church in Jõelähtme was built in the fourteenth century and is one of the oldest churches in Estonia.

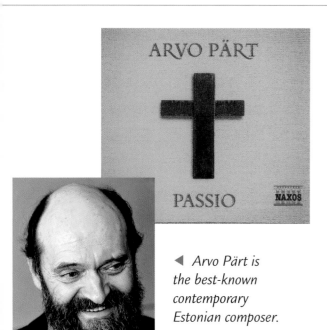

◀ *Arvo Pärt is the best-known contemporary Estonian composer.*

Music

The Estonians love music, and they have hosted song festivals since 1869. These are great celebrations with performances by musical companies, dance groups, and different types of bands from all over Estonia. The whole nation joins together for these events.

Since 1961, Estonia has also celebrated special song and dance festivals for young people. Apart from traditional songs, they perform modern music from contemporary composers. The most famous Estonian composer is Arvo Pärt, who writes beautiful contemporary choir music. These festivals are especially for young people, and only youth orchestras and young musicians and singers are allowed to take part.

Festivals and celebrations

Estonians celebrate Christmas in much the same way as the rest of Europe. At Easter, children paint eggs and, in some families, parents hide presents under their children's pillows. These holidays have only officially been celebrated in the last few years. When Estonia was part of the Soviet Union, the public celebration of Christmas and Easter was forbidden.

Estonians have always celebrated special days according to the ancient traditions in their national calendar. The most popular of these is the Midsummer Day festival, celebrated on June 24. Other popular celebrations are Kadri Day and Martinmas Day in November, when people dress up in costumes and go around singing, dancing, and telling stories in exchange for sweets. People used to believe that Kadris (St. Catherine) and Martinus (St. Martin) would bring a good harvest. Children also enjoy Shrovetide celebrations, six weeks before Easter, when there is usually snow on the ground and they have sledding competitions.

▲ *During the Tallinn Song Festival a special stage is built. The stage can accommodate as many as 24,000 singers at one time.*

▶ *Stamps celebrating Estonian culture, showing people in traditional dress*

Pilleriin and Tina are talking about their favorite festivals. "Midsummer's Day is linked to the summer solstice," explains Pilleriin. "This is a time of beautiful white nights, when there is almost no darkness. Midsummer Night has, for years, been considered a time of wonder. According to legend, it is a time when the fern plant blossoms, and anyone who finds this blossom will become rich, wise and happy. Nowadays, those who are in love go looking for the fern blossom at dusk on Midsummer's Eve."

Tina says: "My favorite festivals are Martinmas and Kadri Day in November. We all disguise ourselves in costumes. On Martinmas Day we wear rags, but on Kadri Day we wear white clothes. We put on masks or paint our faces so no one will recognize us. Then we go from door to door singing and dancing, and people give us candy as a reward."

▲ *On Midsummer Day, people make bonfires and dance and sing around them. In ancient times, people believed the fires would protect them from evil and bring a good harvest.*

Sport

Playing sports is a popular pastime in Estonia, and around 55 percent of the population, both children and adult, takes part in some kind of sporting activity. Since independence, new sports grounds and gyms have been built and old ones have been refurbished across the country. The money spent on sports is considered to be an investment in the future.

The most popular sports are soccer, basketball, and volleyball. There are also several important running events organized every year: the Tartu Autumn Run, the May Run for women, and a Health Run. Popular sports for amateurs are skiing, swimming, canoeing, and cycling. Skiing is the most popular winter sport and many Estonians attend the Tartu Ski Marathon.

Sports are one of the ways that Estonia can bring its achievements and interests to the attention of the world. Seeing the national flag being hoisted and hearing the national anthem being played in honor of an Estonian athlete is a much-prized moment.

▶ *Estonian Erki Nool celebrates winning the gold medal in the decathlon at the 2000 Olympics in Sydney, Australia.*

National symbols

Estonians take great pride in the natural beauty of their country, and certain elements have been adopted as national symbols. The chimney swallow is the national bird of Estonia. It has a bluish-black coat, kite tail, and a ginger throat with white tie. It builds its nest under the eaves of houses. Estonians believe the chimney swallow brings the warm summer weather. In ancient times, they also believed the bird brought good luck.

An old Estonian tale relates the story of a slave girl who worked for a miserly old landlady. She was given too much work and not enough food to eat. The girl turned into a swallow and flew out of the window with a black scarf around her shoulders.

Siret lives on a farm in the countryside. "We have a beautiful garden with apple, plum and pear trees, berry bushes and flowers," she tells us. "My parents raise farm animals. We have a pig, a flock of sheep, a cow, chickens and a rooster. We also have a vegetable garden in which we grow our own produce. My favorites are the strawberries. It's all very good for you."

The national flower of Estonia is the cornflower. This beautiful deep blue-purple flower grows in rye fields across the country – cornflowers and rye almost always grow together. Flour is ground from rye grains, from which black bread is made. This is one of the most popular types of bread in Estonia.

▼ *The 100-crown note shows Lydia Koidula, an Estonian poet and playwright. The 25-crown note shows the writer Anton Hansen-Tammsaare.*

The flag

Even the colors on the Estonian flag are related to nature. The flag is divided into three equal horizontal bands in the national colors. The blue represents the clear sky and a firm belief in the future. The black band represents the earth, the ancient feeder of mankind. The white stands for purity and hope.

The Estonian national coat of arms depicts three blue lions, one beneath the other, surrounded by oak branches, and it is the most ancient of Estonia's national symbols. The three lions have been used since the thirteenth century, when they served as the coat of arms for Tallinn, which was then under Danish rule.

Currency

The country's currency is the Estonian crown (or kroon – EEK). There are roughly 13 crowns in one U.S. dollar. The Estonian crown is divided into 100 senti. Banknotes are available in denominations of 1, 2, 5, 10, 25, 50, 100, and 500 crowns. Coins are issued in 5, 10, 20, and 50 senti pieces, and in 1 and 5 crown pieces.

The banknotes depict famous Estonian people and symbols that Estonians relate to their country, such as the sea, Estonian villages, an oak tree, and the opera house in Tallinn, among others.

Administration

Estonia has 15 counties, which are divided into smaller parishes. There are more than 200 parishes in Estonia. Approximately 30 percent of Estonians live in the countryside, in smaller settlements that vary greatly in size and age. The larger settlements can be home to hundreds of people and usually have a few shops, a medical center, a church, a school and a town hall. However, the smaller villages might only consist of a few buildings surrounded by fields. Places like this may not even have a shop, let alone a school or any other amenities. Today there are many small villages in Estonia inhabited largely by older people. Young people have moved away to larger settlements or to the towns and cities, where it is easier to study and find work.

▼ *This map of Estonia shows its 15 counties. Each one has its own coat of arms.*

Government

Since June 28, 1992, after 50 years of occupation by the Soviet Union, Estonia has operated as a multi-party republic, which means it is run by representatives of a number of different political parties. The constitution under which it operates was established on this date.

The parliament is called the Riigikogu. It has 101 members who are all elected by the population to serve a four-year term. The president is elected by parliament, and holds office for five years. In reality, the president wields little power, and major decisions are made by parliament under the leadership of the prime minister. The prime minister is chosen by the president, but has to be approved by the other members of parliament. All Estonian citizens over the age of 18 are allowed to vote in elections.

The government consists of a prime minister and a number of ministers. There is a Minister of Education and Research, a Minister of Justice, Ministers of Foreign Affairs, Home Affairs, Social Services, Defense, Environment, Culture, Agriculture, Economic Affairs, and Communication, and a Minister of Finance. The prime minister oversees the activities and portfolios of all the others.

In the most recent elections, on March 2, 2003, the Estonian Center Party received 25.4 percent of the votes, and the Union for the Republic (Res Republica) received 24.6 percent. Both parties have 28 representatives in the parliament. There are six other main political parties in Estonia, including the Estonian United Russian People's Party, set up to ensure that the Russian population is represented in the running of the country. The current president (since 2001) is Arnold Rüütel. The prime minister, chosen in 2003, is Juhan Parts.

Education

Compulsory education lasts for nine years in Estonia, between the ages of 7 and 16. Many children are sent to day care centers before the age of 3, and after this they can attend nursery schools up to the age of 7. These are usually divided into classes with children of a similar age.

▼ *These nursery-school children are doing a "newspaper dance." Each child dances to music on a sheet of newspaper. When the music stops they have to fold the newspaper in half and carry on dancing. Those who step off the paper are out.*

Compulsory education

Estonia has a single-structure education system, which means that it is not divided into different types of school until children reach the age of 16. Year 1 begins at age seven, and after Year 9, pupils are allowed to leave school and get a job if they want to. Schooling is divided into three levels: Years 1 to 3, 4 to 6, and 7 to 9. In the first two stages, children are taught all subjects by one teacher. At the third level, different subjects are taught by specialist teachers.

At school, children study several basic subjects, including the Estonian language, math, history, geography, and natural science. As they get older, they also learn English or German from Year 3, Russian from Year 6, biology from Year 7, and physics from Year 8.

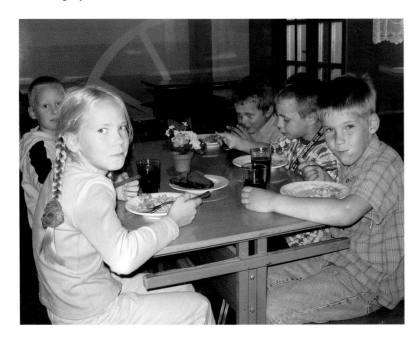

Lessons usually start at 8 o' clock in the morning and end about 2 or 3 o'clock in the afternoon. Pupils have a break for lunch, and most children eat the hot meal provided by the school. Lunches usually consist of roast meat or soup and a dessert. Younger children, in Years 1 to 4, get free lunches. Older pupils have to pay, although local authorities help to pay for school lunches for children from very large or poor families.

◄ *Most schools provide a hot meal in the middle of the day.*

Maret and her classmates are waiting for their teacher to arrive. They are discussing their favorite lessons – most of them enjoy physical education and creative lessons like music and art. Languages are also popular – children are taught English or German from the age of nine in Estonia.

There is a national curriculum in Estonia. This outlines which subjects must be taught and the information that must be covered within these subjects, depending on what level the pupils are at. It gives guidelines for the organization of school time – the number of hours that must be spent on compulsory and optional subjects in a school week. The curriculum also sets achievement targets for each age group. Children are taught in classes of the same age, and there can be no more than 36 students per class. If there are fewer than 20 children in a class, it may be combined with another class to make up the numbers.

School holidays

The school year lasts for just over nine months. It usually starts at the beginning of September and ends in the first week of June. Estonians call the first day of school "wisdom day." During the year, pupils have several holidays. They have two weeks over Christmas, and one week off for Easter. The summer holidays last for nearly three months. In addition to this, there is an autumn holiday – one week, usually at the end of October – and two public holidays, one in February and one in March.

Free time

During the holidays, or at the weekends or evenings, most children like to play outside. They spend their afternoons playing football with their friends, cycling, roller skating or skateboarding. Some children attend "hobby clubs" in the evenings, which are often held at school. Here they might learn music, art or athletics.

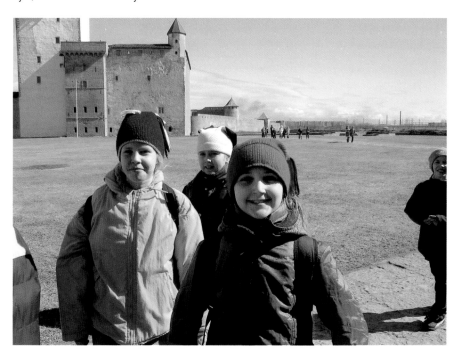

▶ *School trips are often organized to places of historical interest in Estonia. These children are visiting Fort Hermann in Narva.*

◀ Many schools now have computer rooms, or allow students access to computers in their libraries, where children can surf the Internet or research a school project.

Pupils usually have one or two hours of homework to do in the evenings. Once this has been completed, children might watch some television or play computer games. They might look on the Internet and talk through chat rooms – sometimes to friends in other countries. On the weekend, going to movies is a popular pastime for young people. A movie ticket costs the equivalent of about $7.50.

Higher education

After Year 9, students are allowed to leave school. However, there is also the option of going on to higher education in the form of upper secondary schools, called gymnasiums, or to vocational secondary schools. At vocational schools, students will learn more practical subjects to train them for a particular job or profession. Courses at these schools last for three years.

At the age of 19, if they have a secondary-school diploma, students can apply to attend one of Estonia's universities. The most famous of these is the University of Tartu (see page 9), but there are several others, including the Concordia International University of Estonia and the Estonian Agricultural University. Tallinn is home to the Technical University and the University of Educational Sciences. In addition to these, Estonia has a number of academies, where students can specialize in subjects such as music, the arts, or business studies.

Cuisine

Estonians have always eaten what they grow in their fields and gardens, and they use a great deal of fresh produce in their recipes. For this reason traditional dishes depend heavily on the season. Estonian favorites include dark rye bread and dishes made from potatoes, vegetables, and fish.

▼ *Motley dog is a chilled cake made from cookies, cocoa, and jam.*

Recipe for motley dog

Ingredients
1 lb. vanilla wafers or graham crackers
1 cup butter
4 tablespoons cocoa
.5 cup sugar
.5 cup jam

Mash the wafers or crackers and then add the jam. Melt the butter and add the sugar and cocoa. Allow the mixture to cool down and then pour it over the wafers or crackers and jam. Mix and pour it on to greaseproof paper and wrap into a tube. Put it in the refrigerator and leave it there for three hours. Cut the cake into pieces before serving.

Popular dishes

In springtime, Estonian cuisine uses a lot of lamb and veal. The favorite fish of this season is perch, which can be caught in the lakes. Wild leeks and rhubarb are also characteristic of spring in Estonia. Throughout the summer, dishes are very aromatic and contain lots of herbs. New potatoes accompany many meals. By the autumn, fresh berries have been collected and these form the basis of many dishes, especially sauces and accompaniments. This is the hunting season in Estonia, and game is often caught in the forests, including boar, goat and pheasant. In winter, Estonians enjoy eating meat that has been smoked to preserve it for when it cannot be bought fresh. Dishes such as "blood sausage" are served with spicy sauerkraut (pickled cabbage). They drink mulled wine and make gingerbread.

Mushrooms

An Estonian tradition in the early autumn is gathering mushrooms. People have done this for centuries. Families and friends gather together and take trips to the forests, where they hunt in the undergrowth for the different types of edible mushrooms that can be found there. One of the most popular mushrooms is the boletus, which has an umbrella-shaped cap. People have to be careful, though, because some species of boletus are poisonous. Other highly valued mushrooms include chanterelles and milk mushrooms. The Latin name for these is *Lactarius,* and there are about 200 different species. They are called milk mushrooms because when they are squeezed or pressed, they release a milky substance. Some species, like the *Lactarius deliciosus,* are edible, but they don't taste very nice; they have a grainy texture and are rather sour. However, other types have much more flavor and are very popular.

▲ *Mushroom-collecting is a national pastime, and many traditional dishes use fresh mushrooms.*

Viljar is talking about her favorite foods. "I always look forward to my birthday, when my mother makes potato salad, cooks hot dogs and bakes a cake made of cookies," she tells us. "Actually I like hamburgers a lot, but my mother thinks they aren't good for you so we don't have them very often. On a normal day we eat different dishes, including potatoes with mincemeat sauce, mixed vegetables and, of course, pasta. I like mashed potatoes very much. Mother cooks the potatoes until they are very mushy, adds warm milk and diced onion and mixes all the ingredients into a sort of porridge."

Transportation

Estonia has more than 34,000 miles of roads and 600 miles of railways. Both these networks are good, and it is easy to travel around Estonia, and to other European countries, by car or train.

▼ *The Tallinn-Pärnu-Riga highway is the main road from Estonia to the rest of Europe.*

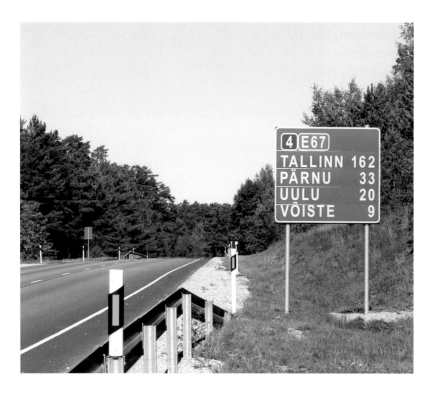

Roads and road signs have recently been improved, and it is now easy for people to travel the short distances around the country. Over the past decade, the number of Estonians owning private cars has increased, and this has seen a decrease in the use of public transportation.

Public transportation

Public transportation in Estonia includes buses, trains, streetcars, and trolley-buses, although the last two only operate in the capital, Tallinn. There is no subway system in Estonia, and buses are the most convenient way to travel around within the cities.

▼ *The European Union has financed many road construction projects in Estonia, greatly improving the transport system.*

▼ *Streetcars and trolley-buses are powered by overhead electricity cables.*

Tee ehitamist rahastas Euroopa Liit
This road was built with EU support

Shipping

Estonia's shipping system is well developed, because so much of the country is bordered by the sea. There are more than 100 ports along the Baltic coast, including Tallinn, Parnu, Haapsalu, and Kunda. Ferries operate between the islands and the mainland.

The largest port, the biggest train station and the international airport are all located within Tallinn's city limits. Tallinn lies 51 miles from Helsinki in Finland, 174 miles from Riga in Latvia, 199 miles from St. Petersburg and 540 miles from Moscow in Russia, 236 miles from Stockholm in Sweden, and 649 miles from Berlin in Germany.

Last winter Pille travelled to one of Estonia's islands: "Do you know how we got there? We drove in our car across the sea on a road of ice! It was quite scary because we could see the ferry close by in the open sea, but my dad said that the ice road is really strong. We even went faster than the ferry!"

◀ From the port of Tallinn it is possible to travel to Finland, Sweden, and other countries aboard a variety of vessels owned by different shipping companies.

▼ Estonia's largest international airport is in Tallinn. The national airline company is Estonian Air, which operates direct flights to many European destinations.

The economy

Since it gained independence in 1991, Estonia has been moving towards a market economy. Many industries were privatized again, and the country sought foreign investment. It became a member of the World Trade Organization in 1999 and this, together with its membership of the European Union in 2004, has helped stabilize and improve the economy.

Industry and agriculture

Estonia is a small country with no major industries, although machines, building materials, textiles, clothes, footwear, and furniture are all made in the country. Approximately 22 percent of Estonia's workforce is employed in these sectors, particularly in the timber, textile and metalworking industries. All these goods are exported to other countries.

The number of people working in the agricultural sector is diminishing rapidly. In 1989, 18 percent of the population worked in farming. Today, this number has decreased to only 6.5 percent. This is largely because of the mechanization of agriculture, particularly in pig-breeding and chicken-farming – fewer workers are now needed in these branches of the industry.

▼ *The traditional timber industry produces lumber, furniture, and other items, such as skis. Furniture manufacturing is the most successful industry in Estonia.*

Milk and eggs are the most important dairy products, and the major crop product is potatoes. The food-processing industry is based on local fish, meat and dairy products. Animal breeding (dairy cattle and pigs) is the main agricultural sector. Mayonnaise, ketchup, mustard, jam, canned vegetable products, and juices are produced in Põltsamaa in the heart of Estonia.

In 1989, over 3 percent of the Estonian working population worked in fisheries. Nowadays the number of fishery workers has decreased to only 0.3 percent. The most important fish harvested in the Baltic Sea are Baltic herring and sprat. Canned spicy sprats from Tallinn are popular outside Estonia.

▲ Tallegg is the largest poultry-processing company in Estonia.

Trade

The number of people employed in trade has grown since the country's independence. In 1989, almost 8 percent of the Estonian workforce was employed in trade. Today, this has increased to almost 15 percent. The key industries involved in trade with other countries are machinery production, wood products, and textiles.

▲ These women are working in a fish-canning factory in Tallin. Here they make the popular export spicy sprat.

◀ There are many textile factories in Estonia's industrial cities. This one is in the capital Tallinn. Textiles make up more than 11 percent of all exports.

▲ *Food-processing is an important industry in Estonia, particularly dairy products. This is a cheese-making factory.*

▼ *Anneke is one of the most popular chocolate bars produced by the Kalev company in Estonia. Kalev was established in 1806.*

Import and export

Estonia's main imports are machinery and equipment, and these make up around 33 percent of all imported goods. Chemical products and textiles are also imported from abroad, along with food products and transport equipment. Estonia's main import partners are Finland, Germany, Sweden, and Russia.

Major exports include machinery and tools, wood and paper products, textiles, and furniture. The main countries Estonia exports to are Finland, Sweden, Germany, and Latvia.

▶ *Estonia's most important exports and the percentages they represent:*

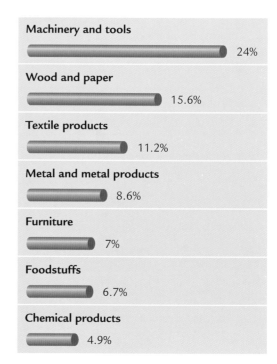

Machinery and tools — 24%

Wood and paper — 15.6%

Textile products — 11.2%

Metal and metal products — 8.6%

Furniture — 7%

Foodstuffs — 6.7%

Chemical products — 4.9%

▼ *The countries to which Estonian goods are exported:*

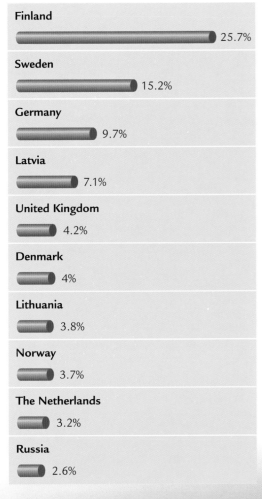

Finland
25.7%

Sweden
15.2%

Germany
9.7%

Latvia
7.1%

United Kingdom
4.2%

Denmark
4%

Lithuania
3.8%

Norway
3.7%

The Netherlands
3.2%

Russia
2.6%

▼ *The countries from which Estonia receives imported goods:*

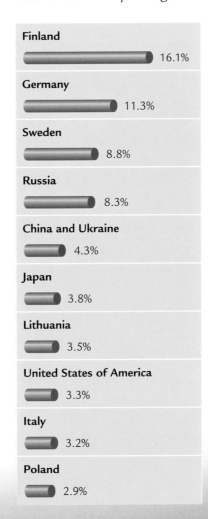

Finland
16.1%

Germany
11.3%

Sweden
8.8%

Russia
8.3%

China and Ukraine
4.3%

Japan
3.8%

Lithuania
3.5%

United States of America
3.3%

Italy
3.2%

Poland
2.9%

Energy

Ninety percent of all Estonia's electricity is produced from the natural resource of oil shale. China and Brazil are the only other countries that use this method of creating electric power (see page 42).

▼ *Oil is extracted from shale in Kohtla-Järve. Once all the oil shale available has been extracted from an area, the mining buildings are moved to a new location and the land is redeveloped.*

Since the 1920s, oil has been obtained from oil shale in power plants in north-eastern Estonia. Oil shale is a natural resource that looks like yellow-brownish coarse sand. The sand contains bitumen (kerosene). By heating the sand to 932°F in an oxygen-free environment, the oil can be extracted. The sand is mined from the surface, so no deep tunnels need to be dug. Energy obtained from oil shale makes up about 60 percent of the total energy needed, and up to 90 percent of the energy produced in Estonia. In some power plants, the sand is burnt and directly transformed into electricity, like coal. Some 4,500 people work in the mines, and just as many work for the energy suppliers.

Oil shale is a fossil fuel, and the only one that occurs naturally in Estonia. It is therefore the only natural source of energy available to be mined. There is no oil or gas to be found in Estonia.

One disadvantage of having to rely so much on oil shale is that large pieces of land are needed for mining, and high levels of waste are produced in the process, which can have a negative effect on the environment. The government and energy industries do all they can to limit this damage and to recultivate the land after use.

◀ Transport trains with huge drums wait to be loaded with oil shale.

▼ In Kohtla-Järve, the factory is located close to the city, and there is usually a smell of bitumen in the air.

Nature

Estonia's natural habitat is richer and more diverse than that of many other countries. Old forests have not yet been cut down, wild animals still roam the forests, beaches remain unspoiled, and swamps have not been drained. Great effort is being made to maintain Estonia's natural beauty.

National parks

One of the main ways the Estonians have preserved their natural landscape is by creating national parks and nature reserves, in which the land, plants and animals are all protected by law. In these areas people are not allowed to pick plants or berries, and they cannot light fires, or interfere with nature in any way. There are four national parks in Estonia, each with a great array of flora and fauna.

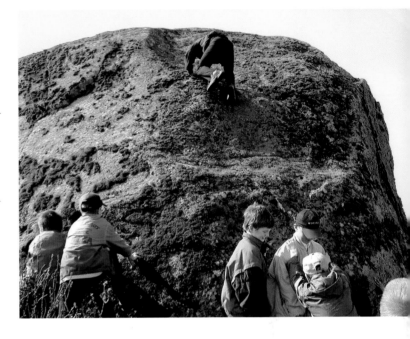

▲ *This enormous boulder, called a "chapel stone," is located in northern Estonia and is a national monument. The stone is 59 feet wide and almost 23 feet high.*

▼ *Estonia's beaches are undeveloped, and great care is taken to keep them clean and free of litter.*

Lahemaa National Park was the first to be established in the Baltic states and is the largest in Estonia. Its name literally means "Land of Bays" and the park is located in northern Estonia, on the Gulf of Finland. This coastal area is covered with bays and inlets, where hundreds of stones were left behind after the last Ice Age. The stones and boulders in the Lahemaa park are all protected.

Some of the park's most beautiful features are its forests and swamps, and these are where many of the rarest plants and flowers can be found. Marshland is often covered by bog moss, which can be 10–13 feet thick in some places. In the middle of the marsh there are deep brackish waterholes or bogs. These marshes are home to many unique plants. In the Estonian countryside and national parks, there are many nature trails, which lead visitors to the most unusual wildlife. Wooden planks are placed over marshes and swamps so people can get across.

The landscape in southern Estonia is protected as part of the Karula National Park. Here, numerous domes and ridges alternate with valleys and hollows, where there are swamps and lakes. In the more inaccessible areas, ancient forests survive, and these are inhabited by eagles, lynxes, wolves, and bears.

▼ *Waterlogged areas like swamps and marshes cover about one-fifth of all Estonian territory.*

▼ *Sundews are one of the most interesting marsh plants because they feed on insects. Sundews capture insects that land on their leaves using the tiny hairs that grow on them. The insects cannot fly away and their bodies are absorbed by the plant. All that is left of the insects are their outer husks and wings.*

The Vilsani National Park mainly protects the offshore landscape – the sea and more than 100 islets off the coast. Hundreds of birds make their homes here, as well as the different plants and sea birds of western Estonia. Some 247 species of birds have been registered in the Vilsani National Park. The most common varieties are eiders, mallards, and seagulls. Other birds, including the barnacle goose, use the park as a stopover on their migratory flights. The center of this national park is a nineteenth-century manor house.

▲ *The hilly domes of southern Estonia are part of the Karula National Park. All the woods and swamps in this area are protected by law.*

The Soomaa National Park is located in the middle of Estonia and was established in order to protect the swamps, meadows and forests that characterize this region – many of which have remained unchanged for centuries. In the summer, there are spectacular river floods in the national park, which cannot be seen anywhere else in Estonia.

Trees and plants

Trees, bushes, and herbaceous plants have played an important role in the lives of Estonians throughout the centuries. They have provided shelter and warmth, have been used to make tools and other goods, and have been a source of food. Estonian forests, fields, and meadows are home to many different species of plants, some of which are quite rare.

The forests in Estonia are mainly made up of pine and fir trees. The most common broad-leaved trees are birches, aspens and elders. Estonians regard the oak – a symbol of strength and power – as a holy tree, while maple trees are the most common trees in parks. The broadest tree in Estonia is a linden, with a girth of 32 feet. The tallest tree is a fir, 148 feet high; the tallest broad-leaved tree is a 131-foot aspen.

▲ *Wild boars can be seen foraging for food in woodland and boggy areas.*   ▲ *Around 4,000 beavers live in Estonia.*

Animals

There are around 80 species of mammal in Estonia. The most common are elk, roe deer, wild boars, bears, lynxes, hares, squirrels, foxes, wolves, raccoons, wild dogs, and hedgehogs. The lynx is the only member of the cat family living in Estonia. It is not always easy to see these animals, as they often come out in the evenings or at night, but they leave signs of their activity all over the landscape. Beavers in particular have come to be regarded as something of a pest, because the dams that they build cause flooding in the forests and meadows.

The bear is the largest predator in the country. There are believed to be around 500 bears living in the wild in Estonia. The elk is the largest animal – an adult bull can weigh up to 1,100 pounds. This is one of the most hunted animals in the country. Roe deer can be seen all over the forests and meadows, and they are also hunted at certain times of year. Estonia has two species of hare – grey and white; they are the fastest animals in the Estonian forests.

▼ *White storks are found all over the Estonian mainland. Here, they appear on a stamp.*

Birds

Estonia is home to various forest, marsh and garden birds, as well as many species of waterfowl. The most common are the forest birds – there are 206 species of nesting birds and 38 species of migrant birds. Birds commonly found in gardens include chaffinches, thrushes, titmice, starlings, crows, magpies, sparrows, and swallows.

The fields and meadows are where skylarks, lapwings, corncrakes, and storks build their nests, while in the forests there are woodpeckers, nightingales, bullfinches, cuckoos, eagles, and owls.

The most common waterfowl are seagulls, ducks, and geese. Cranes and woodcocks live in marshes. The mute swan is the largest water bird to nest in Estonia, and their numbers have increased in recent years.

◀ *A flock of geese. Birds are protected in Estonia, and schools organize trips where the children help to "ring" the birds – they put a small ring round one of their legs, which allows conservationists to gain information on migration and other habits.*

▼ *Signs like this are common on roadsides. In Estonian and Russian, it reads: "Waste dumping forbidden!"*

Environmental issues

More and more attention is being paid to environmental protection in Estonia, and Estonians are happy to help in any way they can. These days, recycling is common. Large waste containers are located in residential areas in towns. People sort their household waste before throwing it away so it can be easily recycled. There are four different containers – for paper, glass, hazardous waste, and plastic.

As well as sorting their trash, other plans are being put into place to preserve the natural environment and avoid pollution. New modern dumps are being built for all kinds of waste – large and small. Modern water processing plants are being built to provide clean and drinkable water and to prevent the rivers from being polluted.

Kaur says: "This autumn I went with my class to collect waste from the roadsides. What we found there was amazing: different jars and bottles, even tires and a shoe!"

Taavi explains how she helped with environmental protection: "I went to Saaremaa to clean the beach. There was a huge amount of litter. People are so stupid. They go there to sunbathe and leave their garbage everywhere."

Eur...

N
W · E
S

DATE DUE

DATE DUE

GAYLORD   PRINTED IN U.S.A.

...land

...blic

...nd

NORTH SEA

United Kingdom

The Ne...

Belgium

Luxemb...

France

Switzerla...

Monaco

ATLANTIC OCEAN

Portugal

Spain

MEDITERRANEAN

0   500 km
0   500 miles